Contents

Preface

Nigel, drunk as usual, walked into a funeral home dressed in shorts, a tee shirt, flip flops, and sunglasses, and drinking a quart of beer. He looked at our mutual dead friend, Grover, lying in the casket, and asked in a loud voice, "What does it all mean?" Although it was an odd moment for all who were present, his question did give us all pause.

What do you think happens when you die? As my friend Hollywood Derusso used to say, "This question is way over my hairdo."

On 9/11 I watched in horror as people jumped to their death from the Twin Towers. Where did they go after they died? Of special interest to me was the lady who made the sign of the cross prior to jumping. Where did she go? Did she merely vanish upon her death? Did she go to a reincarnated state of being? Did she fall into the arms of God? Which god? She had obviously come to a belief there was a god. What was her litmus test for believing in God?

What happens when you die? I certainly do not know. I have my faith, but I do not know with 100% certainty what truly happens. What happens when we die is a marvelous question to ponder. The question allows us to have dialogue and ask:

- Do we merely vanish?
- Do we enter another dimension?
- Are we reincarnated?
- Do we go to heaven?
- Do we go to hell?
- Do we go to a place in between?
- Are we reunited with loved ones and people who were related to us but whom we didn't like when we were on earth? Do they improve? Do we improve?
- Do we become part of the earth in some cosmic way?
- Do we go to another planet?
- Do we all go to Utah?
- Do we all go back to Africa?
- Should we seek cryonic preservation?

- Does it make a difference how we lived our lives?
- Did the choices we make in life impact where we go?

Truly these questions are enigmas.

The man who does not act based upon his own experience is the man to be feared.

—John Locke

Author's Notes

The greatest moment of my life was watching my mother-in-law die. A series of events had slowly played out in my life, and they all came together at her bedside.

Like a moth to a flame, after her death I knew I had found my life's calling. I wanted to talk with people who were in their dying process. I wanted to offer them what comfort I could and help take away some of their fear.

I am unqualified to offer medical or physiological advice. I can only go and talk, listen, and assure them they are not alone and give them a comforting spiritual message. Many times in these discussions I feel I have been blessed to receive a wondrous glimpse into a supernatural reality.

It is difficult to articulate the many wonders I have witnessed. I am careful not to attempt to deal directly with any spirits which may be encountered. I feel this should be strictly left to the ordained or those qualified in this area of expertise. I fully realize there are demon spirits lurking just as there are good and divinely sent ministering spirits.

These experiences have increased my interest in the study of monotheism. I have discovered that the origin of God, not gods, began with the God of Abraham. Judaism, Islam, and Christianity all have their origins in the God of Abraham. I am not a theologian, but my litmus test for God is simple. If there is a watch, there must be a watch maker. If God offers you peace and hope and asks you to get to know Him, and if God's love points you to care for your neighbor, I think this is the God to follow. I find great hope and joy in the promise of Christ because He conquered death.

Although I have many traditional religious viewpoints, I am at odds with many of my fellow believers. The only person I ever physically threw out of my home was a Baptist preacher. During his divorce I offered him comfort, and what did he do but drink up all my liquor, eat my barbeque, and attempt to seduce my wife. He is dead now, bless his heart. No, I did not kill him. However, he personified many of my fellow believers. They are serious hypocrites.

Some of the most despicable people I have known claimed to be religious. But their actions did not in any way mirror those of a child of God.

No one wants to be judged. I hate being judged. Again, too many are quick to condemn, to pass sentence on others without knowing the facts. And one time I had the opportunity to take up for someone who was being belittled by one of those self-appointed judges.

Mardi Gras is a wonderful celebration based upon being joyful prior to the solemn Lenten season. It is tradition that Mardi Gras participants who are Catholic must also give up something in observance of Lent, i.e., candy, television, sex, drinking—you get the picture. I saw a sign one Mardi Gras that read, in jest, "God punishes those who don't punish themselves."

The 2004 Mardi Gras found me walking down Royal Street in New Orleans when I was approached by a young man screaming, "You are hell bound if you don't repent." What an icebreaker, I thought. Granted, I was in costume, but I thought this young fellow's approach and his timing were quite odd, so I engaged him in conversation.

He explained that he was from Minnesota and that this was his first Mardi Gras visit; his purpose in coming was to win souls. I grew more enlightened with every word; he felt that everyone celebrating Mardi Gras was hell bound. So, I told him, "In 1976 I taught in a New Orleans junior high school. There was a boy student there who was a burn victim with severe facial scarring. The other kids were not kind to him, and often called him cruel nicknames. Well, a few years later, I ran into him again at a Mardi Gras parade. Happy to see me and knowing I had always been kind to him, he shared with me that Halloween and Mardi Gras were his favorite holidays because on these days he could wear a mask and no one stared at him. He found so much delight in these costume days that he had begun bringing other burn victims with him to enjoy the festivities—all happily clad en masque. He even joked that, like Cinderella, he and his friends hated it when the clock struck twelve midnight, signaling the party was over—time to go back to being themselves without the masks to shield them."

I looked at the young man from Minnesota and told him, "Sir, you have judged us all without knowing us. My young friend with the burn marks and his friends are somewhere in this crowd. Are they hell bound just for being here?"

The man had no answer. He walked away. And as he proceeded down Royal Street, I yelled, "What are you giving up for Lent?"

As a child, I felt it was the nun's job to put the fear of God in you. I can remember my first grade teacher describing eternity. Sister Veronica would say, "Class, think of the world as a giant marble. Once every year, a large eagle flies around the world and touches its wing against this marble. The length of time it would take for this giant marble to be eroded from the touch of the eagle's wing would still be but a second in eternity."

I recall this teaching as if it were yesterday. And I remember looking up at the giant crucifix which hung over Sister's desk, really wowed by this revelation. Between her explanation of eternity and that ever-present enormous cross over her desk, she had my attention.

One Friday in early November I remember Sister telling us, "God knows each hair we have." I pondered this insight the entire weekend. I could hardly contain my excitement to return to school on Monday so I could ask, "What happens when we get a haircut? How does God react to that?" Having recently learned the work "pubic," I also asked Sister first thing Monday morning, "Does God know about those hairs too when we get them?" I was too young to have them, but I wanted to know what God really thought so I'd be prepared when the time came. Sister sent me to speak with the priest—just like the time I drew a swastika on the back of my English assignment.

Our parish priest was most approachable. He was always smiling; he had kind eyes as I imagined Jesus would have had. This really likable priest would intently listen to my questions, almost always responding, "God wants to be your Father. He wants you to come to Him with your inquisitive thoughts and He wants to reason with you. He loves you and wants you to love Him back." And then he'd end with, "Always remember, Jesus loves the little children. Whenever you come to Him, come to Him like a child, no matter how old you are." I liked my priest friend. Every time we talked, I left feeling good and loved and not fearing God.

Over the years I have come to understand that many people have been molded strictly by fear of God, a fear that flows throughout their lives even until their very end. I find it interesting that the only people who felt the wrath of Jesus were hypocrites, lawyers, and money-focused businessmen who peddled their wares in a holy setting.

Interspersed throughout this book are some beliefs and thoughts that have come to me over the years. Although parts of this book are a memoir, the book is not about me. It is about what we can learn from those who shared their experience of dying. These are their stories. The book is about what we can learn as we approach our own dying process. Sometimes the language can be a bit salty because I use some of the exact words they had used in telling their story. For more than eleven years I have been a hospice volunteer. Each visit is different. Some are eventful and others are mundane. I learn from each experience. For example:

- A lady tells me she sees her dead husband and she isn't asleep.
- A man tells me of seeing water bluer than he has ever seen although he is a world traveler.
- A man screams in agony because he is alone, so alone. Later, he tells me that he is surrounded by friends who died long ago.
- A former English teacher sees colors she cannot describe.
- An eightyish-year-old man hears and sees his father who has been dead for forty years. At first he does not recognize him because he appears to be around nineteen years old.
- A seamstress sees her deceased husband, and she is perplexed as his suit has no pockets.
- A young man is comforted by ministering angels or some type of spirit.

The Ad

An advertisement in a church bulletin reads:

Volunteers needed to visit sick and dying. Experience preferred. Criminal background and drug test required. If interested, call Monelle. 703-XXX-XXXX

"Church office," the voice said quietly and reverently, as if I were calling a funeral home.

"May I speak with Monelle," I sheepishly asked.

"One moment, please," the unidentified voice said.

A deep, smoky voice beamed, "Monelle Nash here."

"My name is Ardie, and I'm calling about the ad in 'The Bulletin' regarding volunteers to visit the sick and dying."

There was a pregnant pause, and then a stern retort, "Why?" she asked, much in the manner of a pissed-off nun, and I *know* what that sounds like.

"Why what?" I asked back.

"Why in the name of God would you want to be a volunteer?"

The smart-ass side of me wanted to say, "I love the smell of human decomposition." But I was nice and said something clumsy like, "I think I have a calling in this area of work."

There was another long pause and a verbal tirade I really wasn't expecting. "You know we get a lot of weirdos that want to apply to be hospice volunteers. We must be really careful to weed out the addicts who want to steal drugs from our dying patients. Then we've got your thieves who want to befriend the poor people who are dying and take advantage of their vulnerability. They steal their money, get them to put them in their wills; you name it and they do it. Then, we have the perverts, the paraphilias. God, don't let me get started on those horrible bastards. Trust me, if you have anything evil on your mind, we are going to find out. Once we had this young, goodlooking volunteer and we found out all she wanted was pills to get high. You aren't one of those, are you?" she asked.

I was rather put out by the manner of her questioning, but I figured she has a job to weed out the candidates with less than honest intentions, so the amiable side of me bit my tongue and the cowardly said, "I'm safe."

Monelle, having breathily taken a long drag on a cigarette, said, "If you truly want to visit the sick and dying, drop me a line on why you want to do this type of work. Tell me about yourself, your religious beliefs and how you came to believe them . . . the more information on your background the better. Also include any information on your encounters with death. After I review what you have written, we will talk."

Dear Monelle,
I think I can best describe why I want to do hospice work by telling you my background. I have enclosed a series of stories which shaped my life and helped create my belief system. I learned a lesson each step of the way beginning with Janice's death and ending with Bon Secour . . .

The Lord has many mansions in heaven …
Some of us will be lucky to have pup tents.

Janice's Death—What's Up With That?

February 18, 1961 was a cold, rainy night—not the kind of night you would imagine there would be a fire. We received a call about 6:00 a.m.

My dad answered the phone, and I could tell from his voice he was getting bad news. When he said, "Oh my God, when is the funeral?" I knew the news was real bad.

My brother and I ran from our beds to our parents' room, jumped on their bed, and asked, "What happened?"

Dad, while wiping the flow of tears from his eyes, said, "Your cousin Janice has died in a fire."

Mom began to sob slowly. My mind raced. Just like most young boys' imaginations would conjure, I wondered if she had been burned to a crisp. I wondered if her dog had also died. My mother secretly knew what I was thinking, but sweetly, her eyes expressed in that nonverbal way that mothers have, "Keep those thoughts to yourself."

Sunday, all the family was invited to come and see the fire scene. I was only six years old, and I could not wait to see what had happened. Secretly, I wanted to be grossed out, but I could not share my curiosity with anyone.

When we arrived at our cousin's home, which we often visited, Janice's mother, a strong Italian Catholic woman, showed us through the charred remains of what had been their cottage-style home.

The walls were still standing, but they were blackened and scorched. There was a strange odor in the home.

When we got to Janice's room, all the walls were also black from smoke. I looked for the pictures of baby Jesus and the Holy Family Janice had placed on the walls—she was a very religious little girl of nine, just about three years older than I. What was so very odd was that the edges of the pictures were charred but not burnt, and the images were not even clouded over with smoke but were rather pristine. Everyone there was dumbfounded by these things, and the family swore they had not been touched or cleaned since the fire a few days before.

Just as strange, Janice had a plastic statue of the Blessed Mother that had sat atop her television, now just a blob of molten plastic on the floor, but only the statue's base had melted and was otherwise just as it was before the fire—there was literally no impact on that image either.

Janice's closet was completely burnt. Nothing was recognizable, but a bookshelf, which held her Bible (singed on the cover, but every page unmarred), and a shoebox that was completely charred on the outside. Inside that box were her personal religious articles—not one of them damaged.

Janice was buried on Monday. Several people in the family, and the funeral staff who were present, all have told the story for years that they had seen a halo appear on the picture of Janice when it was delivered to the funeral home family room so it could be placed on the casket for the service.

Just a few months later, Janice's father was shot and killed by two Italian men.

I began to wonder, "Does God ever send messages or drop hints?"

To Whom It May Concern I Irma Lee Callender was an eye witness to the following:

On or about 02/19/1961 I saw the personal effects of Janice Shipp a minor which died in a fire on 02/17/1961 All religious articles I witnessed were not impacted by the fire which took the life of Janice Shipp.

On or About 02/19/1961 I witnessed the photo which was to be used on top of the casket as My late husband A.M. Cesario obtained the photo from Star Studio in Bogdium, Louisiana. I acknowledge by these presents what appeared as a halo did appear on the photographs.

Signed this date _Irma Lee Callender_ 5/6/14

Melissa W. Bernard - 5/6/04
Notary

MELISSA W. BERNARD, NOTARY PUBLIC
BEAUVILLE PARISH, LOUISIANA
MY COMMISSION IS FOR LIFE

Justice . . . Who Is Capable of Righting the Wrongs?

In was December 1959 and Christmas was just days away. My dad asked if I wanted to have lunch with him. Being a small child, I jumped at the chance. We went to Floyd's, a dining Mecca in the small southern town of Bogalusa, LA.

Floyd's cooked all their food on a well-seasoned flat-iron grill. When you opened the door you were treated to the smell of years of grilling. Seating consisted of a counter where you could watch your meal being prepared. These were the coveted seats. If you couldn't sit at the counter, there were five additional tables next to the jukebox, which was filled with Fats Domino, Ernie K. Doe, and other New Orleans artists. The jukebox was always rocking and the hamburgers were always grilling; it was a treat for all your senses.

Floyd's had two entrances on each side of the triangular building. My dad and I sat next to the east entrance and ordered two burgers with grilled onions, dressed, of course, with pickles, tomatoes and lettuce. Dad had hot coffee, and I ordered a soda.

In those days, black people would come to the east side entrance and stand and wait for their to-go orders. They always went outside to eat on a series of benches under a pecan tree. Being young and naïve, I thought all black people liked to sit outside.

This day, Mr. Howard, a black man who had fought in World War II with my dad, came in. I yelled out to Mr. Howard to come sit with us. There was a strange silence, and my dad had a strange expression on his face. Mr. Howard didn't say anything and he too had a strange look on his face. I was puzzled, not knowing that in 1959 black people didn't have the freedom to sit in restaurants; they had to go outside. I kept insisting he come over when my dad leaned over and said, "You just stay here for a minute."

My dad went to the counter and told them we were taking our order outside with Mr. Howard.

As we were walking out, a man looked at my dad and said, "You dagos need to be with niggers; you're the same." My dad didn't say a word as we walked out with Mr. Howard.

I was a bit confused by the whole ordeal. I thought to myself, "What's a dago? Why are we going to eat outside in the cold when inside, it's warm?"

We sat on the bench, and I was quickly distracted by the wonderful taste of the best burger I think I've ever eaten.

While I ate, I listened to my dad and Mr. Howard talk about the war. "The Battle of the Bulge . . . now that was cold," my dad said.

"I thought I would lose some toes, it was so cold," Mr. Howard said.

I finished my burger and also ate a chili bun. God, it was good.

Mr. Howard and Dad made small talk, and I'll never forget what he said. "One day, God willing, my little boy and your son can share a meal inside."

I didn't understand.

As we finished the meal, Mr. Howard and my dad wished each other a merry Christmas. Each of them shook hands and both of them had tears in their eyes. I thought maybe they had too many onions on their burgers.

On the ride home my dad said nothing. As we got out of the car, he told me, "Son, it ain't right what they do to the Negro. Pray one day things get right."

I didn't understand then what he meant. "Dad," I asked, "What's a dago?"

Do Something

I love Florida. When I was nine, my family and I took a trip to Tallahassee, Florida, and we stayed at the Ponce de Leon Motel.

One night while we were there—it was either a dream or a vision that I had—but a man with a beard came to me—as real as any person could be—and he began to speak to me very seriously. He said, "Your father will die shortly; you must do something to save him." That was all that was said, no more, no less.

I got up, went to the bathroom and was befuddled and very upset by the dream. "Do something," the man had said. "Do something," I said over and over to myself. I thought, "I am only nine years old. What in the hell am I supposed to do?" It's common for kids to fear their parents leaving them, but this was a lot stranger than that. What was I supposed to do?

I didn't tell anyone because it all seemed so unreal, but the next day, when our family went to visit the Shrine of Our Lady of La Leche in St. Augustine, I became even more troubled by the dream. My mother noticed my very quiet, pensive behavior and so I told her about it. Her reply was, "Oh God, nothing strange again from you, Ardie! I just can't take much more of your imaginings."

I must admit I had a very active imagination, but it was almost always related to baseball—often pretending I was a key player for the New York Yankees. Other than that, I didn't have visions or even imaginary friends.

September 10, 1962 was a hot, humid, south Louisiana day. I attended Catholic school, and when the bell rang ending recess, I ran to line up. When you attend Catholic grade school, you always line up and march from place to place. I was number three in line, and as I looked up to Sister Doloreta, I saw it. To my utter surprise, a lock of her hair was sticking out from under her habit. "She has hair!" I remarked to myself. "Is it sinful to look upon her hair?" my mind raced. "If she is not bald, does she also have real breasts?" Oh my God, it was too much to ponder. As we walked, single file, into the classroom, I could not believe what I had just witnessed! I needed to get a grip. This was a mind-blowing experience. Was I the only person to have seen this incredible sight?

My best friend, Liska, could tell something was up, and she whispered,

"Quit acting like an idiot. What's going on?" I had no time to chat; this was too serious to share, even with Liska. Apparently I was the only student at Annunciation who had witnessed the hair of a nun! "Had I won the lottery of fate?" Was this a sign? I thought. It was too much for the mind of a boy. Somehow I knew this day would be like no other.

The rest of the day was typical, until about 2:15 p.m. Then I witnessed another sight straight out of the extraordinary. Father Bordenave was dressed in his priestly clothes and was acting very reserved and very formal.

Father Bordenave wasn't usually that sort of priest. Mostly we saw him in khaki pants and a blue denim shirt. He always had a smile and a swagger. Formality just wasn't his "habit." Even when he was saying mass he wasn't a stuffed shirt of a guy. He was more like Bing Crosby in the *Bells of St. Mary* —a cool priest. But this day he was all business.

Father peeped into the classroom, motioned for Sister. "Oh crap," I thought. It could only be one of two things: something related to the earlier hair-raising incident or someone was going to get some bad news. Instinctively, I knew bad news was about to drop on my doorstep. "Ardie Allen," Sister chimed as she motioned for me to come forward. My knees began to knock. I knew the shit was about to hit the fan. Father moved me out of the classroom and into the hallway. I thought, "Could he know about the hair-showing incident? Could God have tipped him to my thoughts on nunly breasts?" He stooped to look down straight into my eyes, and looking so priestly, he said, "Ardie, your dad is dead."

True to what everyone says when you go into shock, everything goes into slow motion. I began to notice everything around me as if I were seeing it for the first time. The walls, the water fountain—it all looked strange.

I followed Father downstairs to meet my older brother. He was crying, so I knew he too had received the news. We embraced and followed Father to his car. I sat in the back seat as we drove to our grandparents' house. We drove over the Avenue B Bridge and it was as if I had never been over that bridge before. The bridge was so meaningful to me for some odd reason.

My grandparents on my mother's side were second-generation French Canadians, and we called them Mamî and Papî, pronounced mom-e and pop-e. If there was anything important going on, you always went to Mamî and Papî's house. Riding out hurricanes, having family get-togethers, big celebrations—this was where we visited; they were always there.

This was the only time in my life I did not want to go into the colorful little

L-shaped house. I knew it was going to suck big-time.

My Aunt Dody was the first to meet me. She hugged me and we just cried —no words, just tears. My mother hugged me next—just tears too—but gave me an odd look. I am sure she was thinking of what I had mentioned to her just twenty-eight days earlier about my father's death. It then hit me. I had done nothing for my father. I had done NOTHING. What was I supposed to do? But I had not honored the request I had received in my dream.

I found a seat in the living room and just sat and thought deep thoughts. My dad's two sisters came into the room and began to hug. They were so obese that, because of the size of their big bellies, they kept bumping into one another, and they had a lot of trouble embracing.

I watched intently as they cried in high-pitched wails. The scene was actually funny, and, involuntarily, I began to laugh.

My Aunt Dody heard me laughing and said, "Give Ardie some smelling salts . . . he is out of his head." I guess I was a little dingy, but I did think it was funny, watching my other aunts trying to hug and crying like cats in heat.

At 6:00 p.m. the funeral home opened, and we got to see my dad's body. Dad looked strange. He was groomed, dressed, and had make-up on as he lay in the coffin. I really knew he was dead because I had never seen Dad groomed, nor in a suit. I knew at that very moment life as I knew it was over. It was going to be a long night.

At 3:15 a.m. on September 11, 1962 I walked outside the funeral home, full of bologna sandwiches and coca-colas. I needed time to think—time to breathe—time to be alone. I began to pray to God. I asked, "Why, God? Why?" God did not answer. I began to think how a loving God could hurt me so badly. How could He hurt my mother, my brother, and all the many people who loved my dad? I received no divine intervention. I thought to myself, "Is there a God?"

We buried my dad, and I went home from the funeral and called his office number. For four days in a row, I called my dad's office number. On the fourth day of calling, a message came on the line saying the phone had been disconnected.

How true. I too had become disconnected.

Altar Boy for Hire

Money was tight after my father died. The priest felt pity for me so he offered me four dollars for every funeral I attended as the altar server. I attended a lot of funerals from the time I was nine until I was about twelve. I never turned down a funeral. Funerals to me then meant money, not sadness. I did my thing—got four bucks—life was good! I can only recall two funerals which stood out from the rest.

One day, the undertaker, as he always did, asked the friends to go to their cars or leave the room. That was when he closed the door to the viewing room so the family would have privacy with their loved one's body and say their final farewells.

Everything was going as usual; the family and close friends were passing by the casket, lingering a bit, crying, etc. I stood quietly by, holding the crucifix.

Then, this one lady looks down at the deceased and says, "We are not burying Momma with that ring." Another lady says, "Oh yes we are."

Then a shouting match ensued, a little hair pulling, and the next thing I knew, these two well-dressed ladies were going at it on the floor.

The priest and the undertaker assured the women that he could remove the ring or have it buried with the deceased, whichever they preferred. He added, "We can exhume the remains at a later date, of course, for a nominal charge if you decide later to retrieve the ring. We are here to make everyone satisfied."

The ring was removed by one of the men who, I noticed, said nothing.

The only other funeral I can recall is one where there were only two mourners present. I assumed one of the attendees was the deceased's wife; the other was a young man, maybe their son. The funeral staff had to go to a restaurant next door to get enough men to help load the casket.

The two attendees rode with me and the priest to the cemetery. When we arrived at the cemetery, the grave diggers helped unload the casket.

All the widow said on the way to the cemetery and on the way back was, "We always had each other . . . we never needed anyone else."

She, no doubt, was reading our minds. No other words were spoken.

My funeral career came to an end when the priest said I was no longer showing proper respect for the situation.

He was correct.

Interested in Hell? Come To Church and See

Summers in south Louisiana are hot, humid, and hazy. As my friend Mardean would say, "Every day in the summer is a bad hair day. No reason to use deodorant because fifteen minutes being outside and you smell like old fish left in the sun."

I was working my way through college, and the best way to earn maximum income was to do manual labor. One summer I got a job digging ditches and working in the sewer, collecting trash and, on good days, patching streets. To beat the heat, we would begin work early around 6:00 a.m. each day. Each day around 11:00 a.m. we would break for lunch. One day we were near a restaurant when the foreman called lunch. Due to the fact that we stunk, we would always take food to go. As we sat outside eating, one of my coworkers said, "Holy crap, here comes my preacher. Don't curse or say anything vulgar." We all took his advice, and we were on our best behavior. No talk of sex, albeit temporarily.

Preacher Randy walked up wearing a green seersucker suit and white bucks. He was a large man who obviously had not missed many meals. "Is it hot enough for you boys? Remember, if you think it is hot now, just think someone in hell would think this is a cool day. I bet they would love to have a sip of that cold drink," he said as he pointed to Greg, one of his parishioners. "Greg, haven't seen you in church lately. How's your mom and them?" Greg sheepishly said, "Everybody's doing fine; we have just been real busy." Preacher Randy smiled and replied, "Don't go short-changing the Good Lord with your time just 'cause it's summer." "No sir," Greg replied. The preacher was about to walk on when he turned to us all sitting, eating our lunches and asked, "Do you boys think the new niggers are gonna help the football team this year?" I was stunned by his comment. The preacher continued, "I hear there are two nigger families just moved here from North Mississippi. Word is they are big and strong and damn fast."

I could not hold my tongue any longer. "Preacher," I said. "When you walked up, Greg told us to watch what we said because you were his preacher. Out of respect, we did. However, when I hear you use the n-word, I think you are wrong, especially since you are a man of the cloth."

Preacher Randy sternly looked at me and said, "Boy, where are your manners? Weren't you taught to respect your elders? For your information, God Himself has cursed the nigger race. They are only superior in their inferiority. You, son, need to get your head screwed on straight."

I thought for a second as my coworkers looked on in disbelief. I said, "You, sir, are a dumb ass. If God believes the way you do, I don't want any part of your God."

Preacher Randy, now extremely angry, says, "Boy, Satan has your mind. You need to get right with God."

I thought, "Don't think so."

My coworkers gathered around me and separated me from the right reverend. We stared at each other as he entered the restaurant. I knew at this point in my life I wanted nothing to do with God, religion, and all the hypocrites who claimed to work, speak, or act for God.

I Had No Destination, but I Was Making Good Time

In the Bible, after Jesus is found in the Temple, you don't read anything about Him until He became thirty years old. These are the missing years. Unlike Jesus, since I would be unworthy to wash his car if He had one, I didn't exactly go missing, but there were a number of years when I disconnected and spiritually went M.I.A. I may have attended church, gone through the motions, but basically the lights were on, but no one was home.

I developed what I called the eight-hour plan for my life. The eight-hour plan took me through high school, college, and thereafter for a long time. I always devoted eight hours to work, eight hours to play, and the only compromise was for work and sleep. Sleep was a bother because I would fear I would miss some fun. Burning the candle at both ends was my motto, and it described my life and my failed marriage. I used to say, "Now that I have given up all hope, I feel much better." I was known by my friends as Party Ardie.

I was thirty years old and going nowhere fast. But I was making great time . . . or so I thought. I sold my house, knocked around Europe for a while, came back, and prepared for a new adventure. I wanted to live in the mountain west. It didn't matter where, just somewhere out there.

Before I moved, I started living between the homes of two lady friends. Judy lived on the lake, and Karen lived in town. I felt, temporarily, that I had the best of both worlds, and it was Christmas time, 1985.

My two lady friends didn't care I was part-time with each of them. They both had said to me at one time or another, "You are not to be taken seriously, Ardie." Fun was all I wanted. And they too didn't want anything to do with anything serious.

In a twist of irony that Christmas season, each of them started asking the heavy questions: Why are we here? What is our purpose? and After this, what?

To their surprise, I would enlighten them about religion, God, and the Holy Bible. They felt it ironic that I would be delivering any insights from those realms.

Although I had much knowledge of many things religious, I was far from religious. Throughout my life I had studied comparative religions, the various teachings of Buddha, and other Eastern philosophies. I had even taken the E.S.T. seminar.

But it was strange to me that the more I talked, the more they listened. They were amazed, after checking out the info I had given them, that what I was telling them was factual.

Rules were for other people. I did not want to play by any rules. To be told not to do something instilled an even greater desire in me to do that which was forbidden. My marriage had failed, so I had no respect for marriage or even other people's marriages. I was having several affairs with married women.

Once a beautiful woman visited from New Orleans, and what started as a one-night stand developed into a two-year affair. It was so lustful and bawdy that the police were called to our hotel room on more than one occasion. Often, our friendly hotel clerk would simply provide the most secluded room in the hotel so as to not bother the other guests. Each time she would visit, we would check into the Sheraton and do the wild monkey dance for hours, all the while drinking ourselves blind. I never felt guilty for attending her wedding and dating her best friend; the thought never entered my mind.

One Friday Karen called and said, "Meet me at the new Benihana near the Sheraton." I laughed to myself as I drove into the parking lot next to the Sheraton. I did a mental re-creation of the scenarios of my numerous rendezvous there with my New Orleans girlfriend. I went into the restaurant and ordered a drink. Karen arrived shortly thereafter.

I took about two sips of my drink, when, not a voice (that would be too mild) but a "power" took over my mind. It was not the little voice inside one's head that says things like, "Eat that chocolate. She is cute. I need to wash my car," not the voice that tells you what and what not to do. This was more than just a feeling; it was an inarticulate power, which took over my mind. I excused myself from the table and went outside to the cold air of the evening. This "granddaddy" of all powers directed me to my knees in the parking lot of the Benihana restaurant. It imprinted the following message in my mind . . . forever.

"You have talked a lot about Me and My wondrous ways. But you are far from Me. You must decide if you want to accept Me or if you will continue to ignore Me."

Like someone in a trance, I said, "I want to accept You." I began to speak in a manner I have never spoken in before or since. I then began a lightning-fast conversation between my mind and something so beyond me I cannot find the words to describe. It would be like trying to describe the taste of a banana. It was far too strange for words . . . too cosmic . . . too everything. Was God communicating with me?

As quickly as my ordeal had begun there on my knees in the parking lot, it was over in an instant. I walked slowly back into the Benihana.

I saw Karen, and she said, "Where in the hell have you been?" and with a piercing look asked, "Do you want beef or chicken?"

I said almost nothing throughout dinner. I dropped Karen off after eating. I could not sleep. I barely ate. I needed time to think, to ponder what had happened. I drove around for hours in a daze. I went into an all-night coffee shop and just sat in silence.

Near sunrise, I stopped at the priest's quarters next to a downtown church. I rang the doorbell several times before an old Irish priest finally came to the door. I could tell I had woken him up. He was not happy and let me know as much.

"What the hell do you want?" he yelled.

I nervously explained about the encounter with God the night before. I expected an "Amen" or other encouraging words, but instead got increasingly louder anger.

"I get to sleep late only once in a while, and today was my day to sleep! You woke me up for this? Go away!"

Is There Coffee in Heaven?

Grandmothers are special. Of course, mine was extra special. No one cooked better fried chicken or made better coffee than the one we called Mamî. Her real name was Elmere.

She loved coffee strong, and the pot was always on. If you ever needed a good coffee buzz, you knew where to go. When you slept overnight at Mamî's, all was right in the world. I would love it when it rained because I could lie in bed and hear the rain fall off the tin roof onto the oyster shells my grandfather, Papî, had placed under the drain spots. The sound was comforting like no other.

As most people probably do, I only thought of my grandmother as sweet, loving, and saintly. She always attended church; she had her holy pictures throughout the house. In her mind, there were no bad pictures of Jesus—velveteen or not; if it was Jesus or the Holy Family, it was all good. Mamî and Papî always supported the church and the school. Her favorite way to support the church was by playing bingo. She often bought extra bingo cards and would say, "The church needs my help. I will purchase more cards and pray to St. Joseph for good luck." Her thought process was, "Surely the good Lord would reward such wonderful behavior and let me enter the pearly gates."

When Mamî was ninety-one, she had a near-death experience. She said she was visited by Jesus. It was not a pleasant visit. She said that Jesus had a beard and Mamî always hated beards, and to see her savior with a beard scared the hell out of her. But what He said really scared her the most, and it confused her. Mamî said Jesus told her, "Elmere, you are not right with Me."

She asked me, "What did He mean when He said I was not right with Him?"

This was a very confusing matter to me because I thought if she was not right with the Lord, why should I try being good? Because if my wonderful, sweet grandmother, Mamî, was not right with the Lord, what chance in hell did I have? If she cannot get into heaven, there was not a snowball's chance in hell for me to get to heaven.

That night I could barely sleep. I tossed and turned and scratched and itched and thought if all the church-going, bingo-playing, holy-picture-hanging—and don't forget the extra bingo-card-buying—won't get her into heaven, what in the name of Sam Hill would it take to get right with Jesus?

When 8:00 a.m. rolled around, I called my secretary and told her I would not be in as I had an important personal matter to handle that could not wait. Missing work is not something I do—almost never.

I called a preacher. I did not know him, but I had heard him speak while visiting his church. He struck me as a real spirit-filled man, a holy man, a man of the cloth, a man who did not know me, but someone I felt I could talk to candidly. I made an 11:00 a.m. appointment. I arrived around 10:50 a.m., and his secretary offered me a cup of coffee (weak by MamÎ's standards, but coffee).

The preacher was young, tall, and spoke with a Bosnian accent. He welcomed me and asked, "What can I do for you?"

I gave the 411 on MamÎ and her visit from Jesus and his strange message, "You are not right with Me."

The priest was drinking his coffee and smoking a cigarette. He took a slow puff and said, "Is that it?"

I'm sure I looked as puzzled as I felt and said, "Yea, that's it. What's the problem?"

This kind of look came across his face, and he said, "Can't you see?"

I thought about getting a little pissed off because, "No, I didn't see."

He continued, "Your grandmother is trying to work her way into heaven."

I was more confused and asked, "What must she do to get right with Jesus?"

He said, "Your grandmother, by going to church, was getting her ticket punched for her attendance, but she is missing the real message. Your grandmother needs to pray and ask for forgiveness for her sins."

I almost punched him. "My grandmother has no sins," my heart had always told me.

"That is where you are wrong," he said. "We are all sinners in need of a savior. Your grandmother needs to realize not through any works she performs but rather by trusting in the gift of His death for her sins will she get right with Jesus. With a humble heart, tell your grandmother to ask for forgiveness and put her trust in what He did, not in what she can do."

I thanked him for his time and left his office. What he had said sounded so "Baptist," as MamÎ would think, "too Baptist." MamÎ thought all Protestants were somehow all Baptists. I knew she would not buy this message. It would be an uphill battle to convince her that the priest's interpretations would get her right with Jesus.

I went to the nursing home and into Mamî's room. She was watching *Days of Our Lives*, her favorite show. I slowly worked what the preacher had said into our conversation. I could tell she was not buying it. And I knew she wasn't buying it when she turned off the television.

"I go to church. I go to confession. I don't hurt anyone. I live a good life. I buy extra bingo cards. What more can I do?" she questioned. Then she looked at me sternly and said, "Ardie, you are starting to sound like one of those people."

That was code for Protestant/Baptist.

"They come by my room all the time and want me to pray with them, but I say, 'Damn it, I'm Catholic. You don't believe in the pope. And I'm not sure who you pray to.' And then I tell them to leave me alone."

It was pretty obvious I was not making any headway, so as I walked out of the room I said, "Remember, Jesus told you that you were 'not right with Him.'"

I waited a few days before I visited Mamî again. I arrived around three in the afternoon. Everything seemed the same. The place still smelled like a big urinal. What was strange was that Mamî was not watching television. Mamî not having the TV on was almost like not having the coffee pot on. With a smile, she reached for my hand.

She said, "I am right with Jesus. I want you to tell everyone at my funeral that I am right with Jesus. He came to me the night before last and said, 'What the preacher told your grandson was the truth.' I got right with Him right then and there. Everything is going to be alright. Please tell everyone. I even saw Papî. He was so young, so handsome in a beautiful suit with no pockets."

My last memory of Mamî was visiting the nursing home, and she was in a wheelchair sitting next to a black lady who had a tambourine, and they were singing some hymn, and Mamî was surrounded by "those people."

Who Said I Have Left?

I was attending Mass in Bethesda, MD, in the early 1990s. As I was walking out of church, I noticed a small sign that read:

Although the church has yet to make an endorsement, Ivan Dragicevic, one of the visionaries from Medjugorje, will be at the chapel at Georgetown University at 6:30 tonight. Free to the public.

As with Fatima, Lourdes, and Garabandel, I had heard about Medjugorje. Story has it six visionaries have been visited since 1981 by the mother of Jesus in the small town of Medjugorje in Bosnia and Herzegovina. The Blessed Virgin appears to them each day, no matter where they are.

Hum, I thought. It could prove to be interesting. I had never been to the campus and had been meaning to go, so I thought I could kill two birds with one stone—see the campus, and visit with the Blessed Virgin, if I was so lucky.

That Sunday evening was cold and foggy. I parked close to the campus, and walked with my umbrella looking for the chapel. I saw a group of old people walking single file. I thought they must be heading to the chapel. I stopped a student wearing a t-shirt that read, "Why be normal?" to be sure I was going in the right direction. He pointed to where the old people were walking.

I found the chapel, which was packed. The crowd was reciting the rosary. I stood in the back next to a crying baby who wouldn't stop no matter what the mother did.

I heard the sound of planes flying over, as Georgetown is on the flight pattern to what was then named National Airport. I noticed a young man in the very front, leading the rosary. I decided to kneel as we all prayed.

Suddenly, the room became quiet. I looked to my left and the baby had quit crying.

Wow. Then the smell . . . roses. It was as if we were in a garden full of roses. Memories of all the times I had smelled roses ran through my mind. Where's the rose smell coming from?

The visionary turned to the audience and through an interpreter thanked everyone for coming. He said the lady was most pleased that on such a dreary night such a large crowd had come out. The visionary was most sincere when he said, "I don't know why I have been chosen to have this communication, but if you knew what I knew, you would turn to God, repent and love one another."

Then he walked off to the right and out of the chapel. People slowly exited the chapel.

I pondered the experience. What's up with the roses? Is this for real?

Life Starts Again . . . and Again and Again . . . and Again and Again

On March 8, 1986, I found my true love. Like a cliché, our eyes met across a crowded bar; the woman I had prayed to find was finally looking back at me. Her name was Nancy. Nancy was the only child of Taft and Margie. After only a short courtship, I met her parents.

Nancy and her mother waited in the kitchen while I went into the living room with her father. Taft was in his early seventies. He was a retired pharmacist. "So you love my daughter?" he inquired.

"Yes, sir," was all I could say as my throat had dried up and my knees were knocking.

"Are you aware you can't give Nancy everything she wants because she wants everything?" he said as he raised an eyebrow.

I didn't know what to say. Being polite, I mustered, "I will try to make her happy."

Taft stared at me for what seemed like an eternity. "Son," he said, "If you love Nancy, you have to learn to love her mother, Margie too. They come as a package."

Taft died ten days later. The daddy torch had been passed.

As I came to know and love the Nancy/Margie combo, I discovered that Margie loved three things:

- Nancy
- Neiman Marcus
- Life

Margie had grown up in an aristocratic family. She was a world traveler of the highest degree and she often spoke of Cuba prior to Castro.

Margie was strong and had the resolve of a champion poker player. Once, as a child, she came home from school to see her house burning to the ground —after that nothing seemed to shake her cool.

The first time I was alone with Margie, after Taft's funeral, she looked at me and said, "You're nothing to look at; you dress cheaply; but if Nancy loves you, I'll learn." Her forthright manner was refreshing. She said what was on her mind, but oddly, she was not judgmental. As she often expressed, "I leave the judgment up to God."

Margie lived alone after Taft died. When we stayed overnight, I noticed that she left the radio on. I asked her why and she replied, "You are never alone if you can hear the music."

One night, while visiting Margie, and after too much scotch, I made her a promise—"If you ever become too lonely or you get scared, you can move in with us."

We received a call in early 1997 . . . we moved Margie in.

She sat daily in an old gray chair. It was old and ugly, but it was *her* chair. She would sit for hours watching television.

One night in early October, Margie fell while getting out of her chair. She was taken to the hospital by ambulance; x-rays were performed; she was diagnosed with lung cancer, her prognosis, six weeks—tops.

Nancy insisted, "Momma doesn't need to know." With conviction, Nancy said, "We will just make her comfortable." No one ever told Margie she had lung cancer.

We kept Margie as comfortable as possible back at home and for three weeks in an assisted-living facility. She refused heavy drugs. She liked to have a clear head. She was peaceful if we just sat holding her hand.

Margie's condition became worse and she was readmitted to the hospice wing of the hospital. Nancy sat with her mother all day and I volunteered to spend the nights.

Margie and I talked throughout the night. Our conversation, which was normally light and casual, took on a more serious quality. I knew Margie was a believer. I knew Margie prayed. But, I didn't know if Margie was saved.

I thought to myself, "Do something."

As with the events of my childhood in the hotel in Florida, I felt compelled to "do something."

Thoughts of Mamî and her encounter with Jesus with a beard drove me to take a bold step. Awkward and yet driven, I blurted out, "Margie, do you believe you are a sinner in need of a savior?"

She began to cry. I held her hand. She calmed.

I said, "Honey, we are not going to sleep tonight until I know 100 percent that you realize you can go to heaven."

She knew the story of my father, and she knew the story of Mamî.

I said, "Let's pray together, 'Lord, I am a sinner, please forgive me and take me to heaven.'"

Margie repeated that prayer with me; we started saying the Lord's Prayer. I would say a line and she would repeat it. Then, we started singing "Amazing Grace," and we hummed the rest of the verses we didn't know.

Margie began to cry again . . . not a typical crying, but a crying from the depths of her being. In between those sobs she cried out, "Elsie, Elsie!" Elsie was Margie's sister who had died the previous year. They began a conversation and then Margie began to laugh. The room was filled with a spirit, a sensation, a way-out-of-this-world feeling. Then I began to cry—uncontrollably. Margie had entered a state of ecstasy. Her body was earthbound, but it was obvious her mind was in a new dimension.

I am ashamed to say that I can remember the zenith of the high of some recreational drugs, but the high I began to experience in this instance would pale in comparison—it was ethereal. This was the real deal. I felt I was on the edge of a force field I could not enter, but could only touch the edge of it.

Margie was engulfed in the force field. I shared it with her at that edge. I thought to myself about having seen a bunch of smarmy preachers on TV shouting "Hallelujah," but for the lack of a better word I said, "Amen. Hallelujah. Holy shit."

If there was ever a moment in my life I was meant to experience . . . *this* was that very moment.

Like a junkie, I did not want to lose the feeling. Something swept through the room, and as quickly as it had entered it had gone.

Margie looked at me and said, "I am not afraid. I will never be afraid again."

She turned over and went to sleep. She snored loudly, as she often did. I lay down feeling depressed because I wanted to feel that sensation again. "How very, very strange," I thought, "that the greatest moment of my life was watching my mother-in-law die."

Often, spiritual encounters can occur in the dying process that leave the dying person in awe of what is ahead.

Bon Secour

A few days later, Margie had a massive stroke. Her room was dark with the exception of the Weather Channel on TV. There was no volume. Her breathing had become very difficult; her eyes had become affixed upward with barely a blink. She now was unable to speak or hold our hands.

A nurse came into the room and asked, "Have you told Margie it is okay for her to die?" We thought that was a weird thing to ask. The nurse explained, "She may be holding on for you, Nancy, because she loves you so much."

Nancy, now so grief-stricken, had to leave the hospital. Her mother whom she loved so very much was truly near death. She could not bear witness any longer.

A nurse came into the room and she administered medicine under Margie's tongue. I sat holding her lifeless hand. The nurse looked at Margie's upward gaze and asked, "Honey, what are you seeing? Are you looking into Heaven?"

The nurse began relating a story, "My brother died a while ago; we were very close. One night after his death, I was preparing for bed and he came to me—not in a dream, but in a presence. I knew it was him. He told me not to cry because he is with God in a beautiful place. I was so moved that I called my sister in Georgia to tell her. To our surprise, my sister was trying to call me because she had just had the same experience."

The nurse's story was a comfort, which I relayed to Nancy.

At 8:15 a.m., Wednesday, November 24, 1999, Margie was pronounced dead. Margie died with her eyes wide open looking forward.

Margie, the most loyal friend (and patron of Neiman-Marcus) I have ever known.

Dear Monelle,

These stories that you just read shaped my beliefs. At my mother-in-law's bedside in her dying process, the puzzle finally fit. The world made sense, I now know. It is all good, and God is truly at the end if you want Him. I want to spend the rest of my life giving people the comforting message I have come to know. I want to hold their hand, speak with them, give them hope, and take away their fears.

I would consider it an honor and a privilege to be able to be a hospice volunteer.

Sincerely,

Dear Ardie,

Remind me not to ask you what time it is! No doubt, you would tell me how to make a watch. All I needed was a few words on why you want to be a hospice volunteer.

I must say after reading your stories, I thought about how once I had a fire in my kitchen. The fire destroyed everything. The phone was completely melted and everything else was charred. The only thing which survived the fire was a plastic statue of the Virgin Mary. It was weird.

We have a meeting and a new volunteer orientation on Sunday.

See you there.

Monelle Nash
Volunteer Coordinator

People do not want to be told what to believe.

Hospice Stories

The following are true vignettes of hospice visits I have had the honor of making.

No Nukes

Russell was a typical, southern good ol' boy. He worked hard, loved his family, and loved to drink and play cards with his friends. Russell viewed God as this strange man, person, or thing, which he feared would smote him if he did anything weird. Per Russell, "When I mess up, sure 'nough God cracks the whip and puts me back in line."

Russell wanted to go to heaven, but he did not particularly like going to church. He didn't like to get dressed up and have some preacher talk about hell. To hear Russell put it, "Sometimes this place can be a little hellish. I need a little comfort on Sunday, no more damnation discussion."

Although Russell felt it uncomfortable to attend church, he attended on the big holidays—Christmas, Easter, and Super Bowl Sunday (because he always bet heavily on the game and felt a little prayer didn't hurt).

Russell loved Harleys, and one day while driving his bike, a little old lady pulled in front of him, and, to hear him tell it, he "ate some gravel and laid down his bike, going roughly 45 mph."

An ambulance came, and, quite frankly, he was more concerned about his Harley than his side pain. They took him to the emergency room and ran a battery of tests. They decided to admit him for further observation. The accident occurred on Tuesday, and by Thursday morning the doctor came in with the report. The news was all bad. Russell was in stage 4 cancer.

Other than being tired and losing some weight, he had no symptoms. He said, "I was always in pain. Pain was just a natural: indigestion, neck pain, back pain, trouble urinating, and having bloody stools was just everyday life," or so he thought.

Russell's dad was a casual acquaintance of mine. On occasion, we would have coffee. His dad told me about Russell's plight and asked if I would visit him in the hospital to talk with him.

On our first visit, I asked Russell if he had ever felt the presence of God. He thought for a few moments and said, "One Christmas morning, it was weird. We were opening presents and I saw my youngest daughter smiling, and it occurred to me that there must be a God because for a minute I felt blessed and thankful for my kids and the good things—not counting the crap like my wife running off on me—but the good things that are in my life."

I couldn't help but laugh a little to myself when Russell said, "God nuked me for all the mess-ups I have made in my life."

On one occasion, Russell asked me how to get right with God. I told him the Jesus story and that, through a simple prayer, he could get right. After that, Russell would always tell me, "Maybe for you that's how it works, but I am convinced, no matter what I do, that God's gonna nuke me."

No matter what I said or how much encouragement I offered Russell, he felt God was this angry old man that could not wait to come face to face with Russell, and that He was going to smote him first and then forever nuke him.

"Russell," I finally asked him, "what does 'nuke you' mean?"

He said, "You know, fire, brimstone, turn you into salt, give you boils, and then burn you."

He just wouldn't believe my telling him many times that if he would just choose to say that he was a child of God and ask forgiveness, no nuking was in his future.

His dad called me one Friday and told me that Russell had lost the ability to speak and had been moved to Lady of Sorrows Hospice, and that he had written down my name with a note, "Ard cum see me."

Strange as it was, I knew this was one of those very important times that I was being summoned.

Russell was nearing death and ministering spirits were visiting him and comforting him. I knew, full well, that nuking was not in his future.

It was a hot July day as I entered his room. Only the hum of the air conditioning could be heard. Russell's dad was leaning over his bed, adjusting the sheets in an attempt to make him more comfortable. His dad said, "Russell, look here, Ardie has come to see you."

I grabbed Russell's hand and I asked, "Russell, show your dad by squeezing my hand . . . show your dad that God has sent His angels to be with you. Russell, squeeze my hand to let your dad know that you are not alone."

Russell squeezed my hand to the point of pain, and he mustered a faint smile. His dad began to cry softly. I looked at Russell's dad and said, "I bet Russell is seeing into heaven." Russell began to blink.

Russell died the next day.

Once people encounter the other realm, their faith increases and they lose some fear of the dying process.

Screw Guilt

Lincoln was not your typical ninety-six-year-old. He took up smoking cigars at ninety-three. He once said, "Hell, sex is a distant memory, so I might as well take up another vice."

Lincoln was a neighbor of mine when I lived in Orlando, Florida. He had been a world traveler, and in his colorful life, he had amassed a small fortune.

No one knew he was rich until after he died. It was made public that his bequests had gone to several universities.

We used to talk for hours about current events, politics, travel—just wherever the conversation would take us. Lincoln always professed to be an atheist. He said, "Struggle with good and evil—Hell, if there was a god, he would just put an end to evil and good would prevail. There is no god."

I would share my faith with him, but he quickly countered, "Faith, religion —it is all a big bunch of bullshit. Real men and women are not going to put their faith in a fairy tale."

Once, our conversation got on the subject of dreams. Lincoln told me he dreamed every night—never in color, but in grey and black.

Once, he called me and said, "Meet me at the pool. I want to talk."

He looked worried; he never looked worried. "What's up?" I asked.

"You are such a freaking Bible thumper; maybe you can shed some light into a dream I've had for the last two nights? The dream is that I am walking in Chicago and a beggar comes up to me and asks for money. I tell him to go fuck himself."

He continued, "What's odd is that, in 1938, I was walking in Chicago and a beggar did come up to me and that is exactly what I told him to do. I had $400 on me. Hell, in 1938, $400 was a hell of a lot of money. What's also weird is that, in this recurring dream, the man is in color. I can never remember seeing color in a dream, so I took a good look at the man, and I swear and be damned that I think it really was the beggar man from 1938."

He looked at me and asked, "What in the world does the dream mean, Ardie?" He paused, took a puff on his Fuente and concluded, "I guess I should have helped the poor bastard."

It was my chance to be preachy, so I said, "You know, it says in the Good Book that on the Last Day, God will separate His people, like goats and sheep. To the sheep He will say, 'Because you gave to the least of my brethren, you gave unto Me.' To the goats He will say, 'Depart from Me because you did not feed Me when I was hungry and give Me drink when I was thirsty.'"

Lincoln took another long drag on his smoke and said, "You Christians are all assholes. Put people down, that's all you do."

I spoke with his doctor right before his death, and she commented that she had told Lincoln she hated to leave his bedside without anyone else being there with him. She knew it wouldn't be long before he died. But Lincoln said, "Don't worry. Trust me, I am not alone."

Lincoln died the next week.

When someone is in the dying process, they become aware of what truly is important. Bills, petty quarrels, and things don't mean a thing!

We All Know a Janie . . . Some of Us ARE a Janie

I met Janie in Silver Spring, Maryland. Janie was a hard person to like, much less love. If you mentioned her name, the following would be echoed by many in describing her:

- Bitter
- Angry
- Know-it-all
- Opinionated
- Divisive
- Troublemaker
- Backbiter
- Loud
- Sarcastic
- Redneck
- Obnoxious
- Rude
- Pushy
- Crude

Janie, bless her heart . . . truly sucked as an individual.

One night, a dear friend was near death, and I ran into Janie who was a mutual friend of ours, and we sat down and had a drink together. Janie lit one cigarette off the last one and kept on smoking all the time I'd known her. Janie had ten fingers and a cigarette.

She stared at me and said, in a squeaky, sarcastic manner, "You are, no doubt, wondering about Marvin's soul, aren't you, you so-called Christian asshole."

I bit my tongue and said, "Janie, have you ever thought about your eternal destination?"

"What the hell do you mean 'eternal destination'? This is it—hell; and when we die, we become dirt," she quipped. And she added, "In your case, dirt not worth shit."

I paused. Wouldn't anyone who encountered such a soul? And then I looked real deep for some manners, ended up dragging up a little devil in me, and said, "How sweet of you to be so kind."

Janie recoiled from my sarcasm as if I'd stepped on a snake in a hole.

"Aren't you supposed to turn the other cheek if you're really a Christian? I think you are just like all the other smarmy-ass people who claim to be religious, but y'all, by far, are the biggest assholes in the world. Keep your Christian bullshit to yourself. Don't ever go preaching on me, or I will spit in your face!"

Several weeks went by and every time I would see Janie she would give me the finger or mouth for me to go have sex with myself.

A few weeks later, one Saturday morning, my wife got a call from Janie. She asked if we had any oxygen canisters (as if we keep those hanging around our house). Janie said she was having a lot of trouble breathing.

After some encouragement, we talked her into going to the doctor. Then, thinking back on our last visit, I remembered she had looked like she had lost a lot of weight; her skin color was pallid grey, and she just looked in ill health. I thought to myself that surely she had lung cancer.

Janie was admitted to the hospital. She quickly received her diagnosis of incurable lung cancer. The doctor said her time was short.

She told several mutual friends that I was not to come anywhere near her. So I wrote the following note and asked a friend to give it to her.

Your Bad News Can Lead You to Good News

Doctor visit after doctor visit confirms the news: you have a terminal disease. Your time is short.

When all is spiraling out of control, all you have are your thoughts.

No one on this earth, no matter how close they are to you can know what you are thinking, what you are feeling. This time is uniquely yours.

You are at a point of decision. You must make a choice. You must say, "Yes" to God, or say, "No, I will go this alone." No one is going to force you in this decision. God will not force you. God will only come if you ask.

Your life experiences are yours and yours only. You may come to this point in your life with a personal bias against organized religions. You may have been hurt by someone who claimed to be spiritual. You may have felt God doesn't exist or God was always distant and was never truly real in your life.

Back to the decision: no matter the past, in the quiet of your inner thought, you must make a decision.

Remember this choice does not include another human being. No paperwork is required. No money is needed—just your decision to make.

You may be thinking, if there is a God, He could never forgive you for the life you've lived. You may be burdened with guilt for a sin which you committed that you might be too ashamed to discuss.

Think about this: the first person to see the risen Christ was a previously demon-possessed lady. Peter denied Jesus three times, and what did Jesus do but make him head of His church? When Jesus was dying on the cross, one of the men being crucified alongside him asked for forgiveness and was assured by Jesus that they would share paradise together that day.
You see, the only sin which cannot be forgiven is the rejection of God and His Son, whom He sent to die for all of us.

It is your decision to make. Your eternal salvation hangs in the balance. Your dying process may be the introduction to the best friend a soul can have.

If you do choose God, His spirit will be with you forever.

Although your remaining time may be difficult, His presence will be with you at the end and always.

It is your decision to make.

Janie died two days after reading my note. She was cremated, and there was to be a small service held in a small chapel.
To my surprise, that chapel was filled to standing-room only. Everyone there, it seemed, agreed that Janie was difficult. But there was an underlying feeling that there was an unusual goodness about her.

At the funeral, we learned that she was given up by her parents at birth. She had experienced a hard life with chronic health problems and bigger money problems. She had been married three times and two of her husbands had died at a young age. She had dreams which were never fulfilled. She had plans which were never brought to fruition.

We all learned that Janie had called for a priest prior to her death.

God reads hearts. He can see right through mockery.

Don't Commit Crepe Murder

Linda was my scientist neighbor when I lived for a while in Jersey. She was not all that friendly, but she had a beautiful yard, which was meticulously manicured; and I admired it and her passion for gardening. Linda loved things being orderly.

I once offered to prune her crepe myrtles, and she replied that I may do so when there was a cold day in hell. You see, she didn't know that I was from the South and that I knew what "crepe murder" is. Moreover, her garden was an expression of herself and she didn't want anyone messing with it.

Linda, who was about the same age as I, was diagnosed with a brain tumor in early 2000. Her mother moved in with her to care for her.

Linda, being the consummate scientist, had little regard for that which cannot be explained in less than scientific terms.

Weeks before Linda's death, I mustered the courage to ask her mother if I could speak with Linda about the Lord. Her mother's reply was, "To what Lord are we referring?" After I explained that I had a rather unique mission, she respectfully declined my gesture.

Her mother did make an odd comment, though. She said, "Although we are not believers in your Lord, we do have some good luck charms." So, I asked to see the lucky charms, and her mother went in her home and returned with a rosary and a picture of the Madonna and baby Jesus.

I respectfully explained that these were not good luck charms but sacred objects. My comments were dismissed—the same reaction as when I had offered Linda tips on growing Big Boy tomatoes. The point was that I hoped that her mother would go inside and tell Linda that she actually had some holy items around her. Maybe that would get her to thinking beyond the scientific box.

Three days prior to Linda's death, I saw her mother taking out the garbage. I approached her and gingerly asked about Linda's well-being.

Her mother replied, "It is only a matter of time."

I thought it might be a good opportunity to give her mother a basic prayer book about understanding God. I myself had gotten the book from a group that comes to Mardi Gras each year in order to harass revelers and proclaim all to be hell bound, although none of them probably grew up with the Mardi

Gras tradition. But I digress . . .

Linda's mother was too tired to argue or engage me in a philosophical discussion on Darwin and thus accepted the book.

It was a cold but sunny New Jersey Sunday when Linda died in early March around 8:30 in the morning.

A small crowd had gathered in her front yard to offer condolences. Around 11:30, the coroner arrived to remove her body. About 3:30 that afternoon, the backyard went into full bloom.

Dogwoods bloomed, narcissus sprang up; forsythia popped out in yellow beauty. The whole neighborhood was abuzz over the strange occurrence of the garden spectacle long before its season.

Linda's part-time landscaper, Chris, himself a Baptist preacher, was called to witness the amazingly glorious site. He kept saying, "I was here Friday and everything was dormant. This is odd; very odd . . . is this a sign of some sort?" It was indeed.

Linda's body was given to science. Chris visited the garden each day as if visiting a shrine. Two weeks later, the forty-six-year-old gardener/preacher died of a sudden heart attack in Linda's backyard.

I Will Run and Play Forever

Zollie was stricken with multiple sclerosis when he was eight years old. He was the only child of the Bantams. Mrs. Bantam drew strength she didn't know she had from her little Zollie's infirmity. With the greatest of love, Mrs. Bantam began a dedication of her life to the care and happiness of her precious son.

I met Zollie and his mother when he was forty-four years old. After thirty-seven operations, all unsuccessful, Zollie weighed roughly seventy-five pounds, and his body was contorted as he laid permanently in bed in a fetal position. Zollie and his mother had a rather esoteric communication system. Zollie couldn't utter a word, but he made guttural sounds which his mother understood. The boy, now grown to only a hint of a man's size, had never gotten to play as a child, but Zollie loved football. A large poster of Terry Bradshaw hung over his bed.

On my first visit with them, and after a long conversation with his mother, she said, "Zollie, we are going to pray now." Zollie folded his hands together, and after his mother and I had prayed, I said, "Amen." Zollie uttered his version of "Amen."

For several months, I went to call on Zollie and his mom. One day she called me and said, "Please come pray with us. I think Zollie is nearing the end." I rushed to their home; the hospice nurse was there as I walked into the brightly-lit room. The scene was just angelic . . . ethereal . . . it was not of this world. It seemed as though the Lord's presence was there completely. I began to cry. But these were not tears of sadness. The hospice nurse was already crying too. No, it wasn't a sad feeling we were experiencing, but a feeling that the spirit of God was surrounding all of us.

Mrs. Bantam looked at us, puzzled, "Why are y'all crying? He is going to a better place." The hospice nurse replied, "Zollie has already begun to experience God's welcoming party! Ardie and I feel blessed to share the spirit in the room." But Mrs. Bantam didn't really seem to understand and there just really aren't words to explain.

Zollie died that evening. Eleven people attended his funeral. The preacher who gave the eulogy summed it up simply, "In God's kingdom, Zollie will jump and run and play forever, in God's presence."

All who were there chimed in unison, "Amen. Amen."

Some people wonder if their life has meant anything.

The Blue House Was Not Blue

The Wilson's house had seen better days. The paint was fading from its original blue color, and the remaining paint was peeling. It was a very quaint home in spite of its age and deterioration. As I entered, it had a unique smell as other people's houses tend to do. Theirs generally smelled like apple pie, but depending on where I sat, I also got a whiff of urine.

Mr. Wilson welcomed me in and offered me a soft drink. I explained that Mrs. Wilson's church had sent me to offer her Holy Communion.

Mr. Wilson motioned for me to sit down to wait for her. I could hear someone in the next room rolling around and lightly singing. I assumed that voice was Mrs. Wilson's, but she didn't seem to have any sense of urgency to come to see who had arrived.

After a few minutes of small talk, Mrs. Wilson yelled from the other room, "Are you the man from the church?"

I said, rather loudly, in turn, "Yes."

She yelled again, "We just celebrated our fifty-fourth wedding anniversary!"

I was told that Mrs. Wilson had been suffering from Alzheimer's disease for several years. But it didn't appear that was the case from her voice from the other room.

Then, as an actress might make a gracefully grand entrance, Mrs. Wilson wheeled herself into the living room. She was meticulous in her appearance —her dress neatly pressed, nails painted perfectly, bejeweled, and perfumed. Now she was finally ready for company.

She blurted out, "I am Rosemary Alice Wilson, and I have been married for fifty-four years to this most wonderful man before you. He is a doll, a prince of a man. I have been sick for a while, but now I am much better."

Although I tried to interject something into the conversation, Mrs. Wilson let me know, with her whole doyenne presence, that she was going to do all the talking. And, I was only there to listen.

"Let me tell you about my sickness and the day I got well," she said. "I don't know what you know about dementia or Alzheimer's disease, but, for me, it was like I could hear, but when I spoke, it was not what I wanted to say. It was like someone or something took over my brain. I felt I was responding to what was said weeks earlier, and I was just getting around to answering. Get it? I was not quick. Slow was I. Do you get it? Slowwwww. Gerald, tell the man I used to be quick; I wasn't so slow."

Mr. Wilson nodded and said a bit timidly, "She used to be fast; that's right."

Mrs. Wilson muttered, "This one day I woke up and I started crying because I realized I was no longer quick. Then, all of a sudden, I was transported to a beautiful place . . . prettier than California . . . prettier than Hawaii. This place had mountains, water—the most beautiful water I had ever seen. The colors were out of this world, I tell you, the brightest colors you have ever seen: purple like you have never seen, golds so gold they were almost like light. Lordy, I tell you they were beautiful." Getting more enthusiastic with each word, she said, "It was like I could fly like a bird; and I was flying, looking over this valley. I then swoop down to the valley below, and under my feet is pine straw. I love the feel of pine straw on my bare feet —sand and pine straw are my favorite things to walk on barefooted. I then hear a voice which says, 'Do not be afraid to come to me.' I take the first step, as I go forward. Then I am transported—whoosh!—and then I am looking at Gerald.

"He is looking oddly at me, and I said, 'Gerald, please get me a cup of coffee and chicory, with a little cream, would you, honey? And, maybe some wheat toast with a little mayhaw jelly.'

"I noticed Gerald beginning to cry, and he said, 'Alice, is that you?' I said, 'Gerald, I am back. Was I gone long?' He said, 'Alice, it has been five or more years since we have had our coffee and chicory together.'"

Alice looked at me and said, "What do you think?" I was at a loss for words. I looked at the older couple and said, "I have no idea."

Alice said, "I think I went to Heaven. But I am back now. If it wasn't for Gerald and my grown children, I would have liked to have stayed in that beautiful place." She paused, "But I am back."

Gerald looked lovingly at Alice, and she told the story again. Before I left, she told her story three more times. She didn't recount the story because of a lack of memory; she told it again and again and even asked me to please tell her story to others.

As I left, the last words I heard were, "more beautiful than Colorado."

Gerald died a month later. Alice died in a nursing home six months after that.

The doctors said that the dementia had returned.
I was told that her last words were, "It is so beautiful."

I Guess I'd Settle for Peace

Lee was a World War II pilot. He flew thirty-six missions over Germany during the war. The war had defined his life. He had been a daredevil all his life. He loved to live on the edge.

When I first met Lee, he was eighty-one, bedridden and legally blind, and he said, "I'm dying of something." But he still was the kind of guy who was tough as a boot.

Lee drank a bit. As he quipped, "I only drink when I am awake."

Lee lived alone—except for his sitting service du jour—in a beautiful Victorian home off Monument Avenue in a lush, tree-lined, historic part of Richmond, Virginia. He had 24-hour care from various sitting services. All day long he sat in his adjustable bed. His room was filled with WWII flying memorabilia. He always wore a red baseball cap, and he always had classical jazz or be-bop music playing gently in the background. Lee would sing along on occasion. He could easily have been a member of the tone-deaf choir. With all his talents, singing in the proper key escaped him.

Lee's son had called the church and asked if a volunteer could come by from time to time to visit. His son had said to the church screener that his dad was dying. Lee was dying, but his time was not short. I got the call and took the assignment.

On my first visit, I walked into his home after a brief knock. The smell of urine from his colostomy bag was overwhelming. He looked crusty, and his initial attitude was cynical.

Lee's first words to me were, "Are you a do-gooder from the church, sent to save my soul?" I retorted, "From the looks of things, and from what I have heard about you, my friend, you are a lost cause." He smiled and said, "Have you ever seen a man burn to death?" Sheepishly I said, "No."

Lee took a sip of his drink. That day it was vodka and tonic—95 percent vodka, 2 percent ice, and 3 percent tonic. Lee was very exacting on details. He loved to paint a picture. An exact picture.

Lee then looked up, and it was if I had put an audio book into a player. He began: "My plane was called the Black Dragon. We were taxiing down the runway prior to a practice mission. I gazed to my left and noticed three soldiers were arming a plane off to the side of the tarmac. Suddenly, there was an explosion. It shook the Dragon. As I looked over to where the men had been, one man had been blown a hundred to two hundred feet into the air. Like a ragdoll, he fell to the ground in pieces. Another of the men was on fire. It appeared he was trying to walk forward—two, maybe three steps forward. He was a fiery mess. I could not take my eyes off the poor bastard as he burned and then fell lifelessly to the ground. I never saw the other soldier. No doubt, he was blown to bits."

It was pretty obvious Lee was testing me. I really wanted to vomit because Lee was so graphic in his description. But I got a grip, and said, "Cool story."

Lee said, "If you like that story, I have a million of them." He continued, eager to wear me down.

He told stories of attending the Nuremberg trials in post-WWII Europe. He had commandeered a Horch vehicle, owned by one of Hitler's field marshals. Lee said, "The girls loved my car. When I drove the Horch, I was King Damn Kong."

He loved talking about women he'd known, but not quite as much as he loved talking about his military days and the honor of serving his country.

I asked him that day if he didn't just want to feel peaceful, not riling himself over the stories of blood and battles. "I guess I'll settle for peace." And in the next breath, as he straightened his back as if the hair on it were standing up, questioned, "Have you ever heard of the memorial at Maastricht in the Netherlands?"

I said, "No."

He then proceeded to tell me, "After the War, a large cemetery was placed near Maastricht. I drove up to the site in my Horch and heard a strange sound, a sucking sound. I asked the commanding officer about the sound. He looked at me, annoyed that he had to answer the question. 'We have sixteen thousand new bodies to be entombed. What you hear are maggots.'"

Thus began my four years of visits with my pal Lee.

I was given a key, and I would let myself in the back gate. We would talk for hours, depending on his mood and his alcohol consumption.

Once I asked Lee if he was ever scared during the war. He paused, took a sip of his vodka and lime—99 percent vodka, 1 percent lime—and said, "No, no. Hell, I loved being a pilot. I felt 110 percent alive when I was flying. And, if they were shooting at us, it made me 125 percent alive. I had a routine. I would fly my mission, get my crew home safely. I would then get drunk, get laid—like I said, I was King Damn Kong."

As he continued, his facial expression turned much more serious, "Oh, I got smoke in my drawers once. We were on a bombing mission. We seemed to be receiving flack from every direction. We took a hit, and then cold air began to rush into the cockpit. All my gauges went to hell. The words just blasted from me as I cried out, 'Oh, my God!' My copilot was praying out loud. But something very weird happened after I cried out. A presence filled the cockpit. A calming presence came over me. I was able to maneuver the plane back—but, by the grace of God."

This was Lee's first mention of God in our discussions. Lee said, "I didn't know what the presence was, but it saved me and my crew."

That night, as I was walking out, Lee paused and said, "Laddie, that presence has been with me since that night. Next visit, I will tell you about it if you'll bring me some Stilton cheese."

I could not wait for our next visit. So the next day, I left myself in, only to hear Lee singing along with Louie Prima, "Just a Gigolo." I just sat and watched in awe as he badly sang along with the recording of the fun song. Thinking to myself that the day's vodka and no ice were kicking in, I yelled out over the music, "Lee, it's me!" He quickly turned the music down and said, "Glad you are here. Sit back. I want to tell you something."

I was always eager to hear Lee's stories.

He began, "Do you remember last time I told you about the presence coming into the cockpit, and I told you that presence has been with me ever since that night? Well, I have news for you. A few days ago, right after I woke up, I was sitting in the bed, and the housekeeper brought me a cup of coffee. After a few sips, I saw standing at the foot of my bed four soldiers in full uniform. I instinctively knew they were angels. So, I asked them if this was my day they were going to take me home. One of the soldiers said, 'No, not today.' I don't know what possessed me, but I asked, 'Which one of you came the night I cried out in the cockpit?' One of the soldiers stepped forward, gave me a salute, and said, 'That was me, sir. I am your guardian angel.'"

Lee paused as he looked now, directly into my eyes, "What do you think of that, Ardie?"

Groping for words, I said, "Pretty cool."

Lee asked, "Do you think you see your friends in heaven?"

So I told Lee what I think about heaven.

Lee sank into a depression for several visits. He seemed distant and was not as graphic in telling his tales.

Two weeks before he died, I walked in and I woke him up. I asked if I should come back at another time, and he said, "Heavens, no." In fact, he begged me to please stay because he had something to tell me.

This day Lee was not drinking. He straightened himself upright in the bed and said, "Laddie, when I go to heaven, I am going to see all my friends who made it through the war, and I know I won't be able to remember the ones that didn't."

I asked him how he came to the knowledge that he would be seeing familiar people when he got to heaven.

"Yesterday morning," he said, "I was having my first cup of coffee, and I was transported to a beautiful place. It was more beautiful than the Alps. The water was more beautiful than the Mediterranean. The colors were not any colors I could describe. I saw a young man sitting by the edge of the water, apparently fishing. I asked the young man if he was having any luck. The young man said, 'Lee, I am just playing.' I asked the young man how he knew my name. That young man hesitated and then said, 'Lee, I am your father.' Then I laughed as I told him, 'You look nineteen!' The man who said he was my dad told me, 'In heaven, we all look young, Lee. When you come to heaven, we have young bodies. You will have your body when you were at your best. And your friends are awaiting your arrival.'"

Lee looked at me and said, "I am not depressed anymore."

I knew Lee's time was short. Before leaving, I told Lee, "My friend, it has been an honor and a privilege to visit you. You are the real deal; you are a hero. Thank you for what you did for our country. If it had not been for you and guys like you, we all could be speaking German today." Lee laughed slightly and with a whisper, he said, "The Germans make great engines. You can't beat their cars. I am sure glad they are not our enemies anymore."

At Lee's funeral, several people spoke of his bravery. I learned he flew a crop-duster for fun, and he donated all of the money he made to charity. I also learned he raced cars competitively well into his seventies.

Lee was a true man's man.

Friends are very important. They are often the family of choice.

Chihuahuas I Have Known

Giselle loved Chihuahuas. Others often have a disdain for the little nervous dogs, but she could not get enough of them. She would say, "My heart goes out to the little ugly creatures, someone's gotta love them."

Giselle spent a lot of time caring for the little dogs and helping hungry humans. Although Giselle had modest means, she was always seeking ways to help others down on their luck. She would sacrifice to raise money to buy groceries for neighbors and those she heard were in need of a hand. If asked about her calling to care for others, she said, "If I help others, it always comes back a hundred times."

Giselle was like most hard working people of the Bayou country of South Louisiana. She put great effort into raising her family, giving them oodles of love, and caring for her fellow man. And she loved to have a good time. Her idea of heaven was a jukebox and a dance floor and lots of friends and family.

My first memory of her was watching her dance at Salt Bayou, with her happy-go-lucky husband and her daughter who was no more than a baby. Giselle's favorite holidays were Christmas and Mardi Gras. She also loved the seasons . . . crawfish season, crab season, and football season. She would often joke, "Louisiana has only two weather seasons, summer and February." If ever there was the epitome of someone with joie de vivre, it was Giselle.

She had a special devotion to St. Francis of Assisi, the patron saint of animals. She also cherished St. Thérèse, known as the little flower of Jesus because she had once read St. Thérèse was full of playfulness, a quality they most certainly shared.

Throughout Giselle's life, she offered sacrifices to her favorite saints to appeal for their help when there were health problems, family issues, and other concerns.

She was devout in her love of God. If you knew Giselle, you loved her. There were literally no in-betweens.

When her friends and family learned she'd been diagnosed with cancer, they all rushed to her aid as she had rushed to help them and so many others.

One friend, Mr. Bush, had a rosary he had brought home from Medjurgoje where patrons believe the Blessed Virgin has been appearing since 1981. Mr.

Bush gave the rosary to Giselle to pray with during her illness.

Although it is a common phenomenon of the apparition that sacred objects brought from Medjugorje often changed to gold. What was so beautifully extraordinary was that it happened one night as Giselle was holding it while she prayed. If the rosary was going to turn gold for anyone, it would for Giselle.

Giselle and her husband often went to church on Saturday so they could sleep late and watch the Saints play at noon on Sunday. One Saturday Giselle, her husband, and her sister, Lee, went to Mass. Just before Mass began, Giselle whispered to her sister that she wished she had a rose to place on the altar next to the statue of St. Francis since the church seemed a bit bare without many flowers.

Just then, Lee opened the church bulletin she had picked up on the way into the church, and out of the bulletin, a plastic rose fell at Giselle's feet.

When Giselle saw the rose, she laughed. She thought truly St. Thérèse was sending a playful message of sorts since the little flower of Jesus had issued to her "a tacky plastic rose, but a rose nonetheless."

After her diagnosis, Giselle became bedridden very quickly. She asked her family to come and pray with her. She let everyone know she had decided to offer up her pain as a sacrifice to the Lord she loved. As Giselle said, "I think it would please God if I offered up my suffering."

Giselle, in her death process, began to see her mother and her father. The last few days of her life, she could not speak. Her family encircled her and prayed and Giselle's daughter, through tears, said, "Momma, don't hang on for us. Be with God."

Giselle seemed to smile as she died. She was buried on Mardi Gras day.

I was honored to perform her eulogy.

If there is money associated with something, most likely that something is not associated with God.

Love Just Will Not Die, but I Think I Will

Joseph was a hard working man, a man of few words, but strong in his deeds. Like a lot of good people, he raised his family, paid his taxes, and helped his fellow man whenever he could. He wasn't perfect, he liked to toss a cold one back and pull a slot machine every now and then, but otherwise, he lived on the straight and narrow. He would take a bullet for any of his kids; he could correct them, but in his eyes, they did no wrong—ever. He liked to keep a clean yard, and his house was always the neatest house in the neighborhood. His yard was a symbol of his life: neat, clean, and orderly. He could control the things in his realm, but he could not control what he felt was the mess in the rest of the world.

When others fell on hard times, he would help out whenever he could. He wasn't about fanfare, just action. You could always count on Joseph.

When his wife of fifty-six years died, he thought he could handle it, but he could not. He never lost his faith, but he just could not be alone. He began to develop a series of ailments: shingles, diabetes, and gout. His kids tried to offer him comfort, but nothing could take the place of his wife.

Joseph had endured hurricanes all his life—literally: Betsy, Camille, Hilda, Bob, you name them and he endured them and took pride in being the first to clean his yard after the tempest.

He was not ready for Katrina; things were going to be different and all bets were off. He started off like everyone else the night before the storm. He had his flashlights; he had his water; he was also expecting to lose power as he had in all of the storms before, so he had his generator all ready to go too. As Joseph would say, "Just have faith, it's going to be bad, but have faith."

The Monday morning of Katrina, a series of imbedded tornadoes passed around. A falling tree crushed his car, but lucky for him, none fell on his house.

He and his sister-in-law had ridden out the storm. After about eight hours, it had finally blown through, and they went outside to take a look. They were amazed at the extent of the damage. It was as if God had smote the land. Trees were down everywhere; many houses were crushed.

Although the water had risen, flooding, luckily, was not going to be a problem in their area. People were walking around, dazed by the destruction.

This time, Joseph was not going to win the contest for the quickest yard cleanup because a big tree had landed in his front yard too.

Joseph quickly took control, assessed the damage, and as always, found the neighbor in greatest need and offered him his generator.

The first night after the storm was spent in darkness, the humidity was oppressive, and the world around them had begun to smell.

With the help of the National Guard, I was able to get to Joseph at daylight. I walked into his home because all of the doors and windows were open to combat the heat and humidity.

When I saw Joseph, he was sleeping. I said, "Are you ready to take a ride? A road is cleared, and we can head north to Shreveport." Without hesitation, he said with his own bit of humor, "Do you have air conditioning?" I really did think he might die on me before we could get out. He furthered my silent fear when he said, "It is probably a good idea for us to go because I need to keep my insulin cool and we are running out of ice."

All his children agreed it was best too. They were young and had generators, and they thought the worst was over.

What I did not tell Joseph was that I was running out of gas. It was highly unlikely we would make it all the way to North Louisiana because on the way down, gas had already become very scarce. As a matter of fact, I had been harassed on the drive down by some people fleeing New Orleans who needed gas. The interstate was lined with cars out of gas, like a big parking lot. I thought I would share this tidbit of info later and well en route.

We were in awe as we passed through Washington Parish and into Mississippi. The ruination was intense. Katrina was unlike any other storm, simply because of the width of its path. We were well inland, almost one hundred miles from the coast, and we were still in the impacted area. Cars littered the highway—all out of gas.

It appeared the western end of the storm was in the McComb, Mississippi area. As we left McComb, the damage was much less.

Approaching Natchez, I felt it was necessary to mention to Joseph that we were running out of gas. It was hard, but I finally said, "Joseph, we will most likely not make it to Shreveport with the gas we have. It is doubtful we can find a hotel or motel with all of the evacuees."

He stared at me and blurted, "Have faith, just faith. The Good Lord will provide."

I did not share Joseph's optimism; I was positive we were going to run out of gas, just like hundreds of other people, which meant that we were going to end up sleeping in our cars. We did have bottled water; I thought, "At least we will not be thirsty."

But knowing Joseph, he would give it all away if he saw someone in need. I didn't tell him that we had an extra case in the trunk. We stopped at gas station after gas station and were consistently flagged off by the signs, "No gas. No idea when we will. Please don't ask. Bathroom out of order."

I slowly began to freak out. I tried to be cool, but I was tired, hungry, sleepy, and hot. The thought of sleeping in a hot car was not my idea of fun.

We crossed the Mississippi River at Natchez and we were back in Louisiana. We stopped at a Burger King in Vidalia. By now, I was freaking out, but Joseph was still cool as a cucumber. He reminded me that we had not had our coffee for the day, although it was three o'clock in the afternoon.

The parking lot was filled with Katrina evacuees. We went to the restroom; then we ordered two large coffees and two hamburgers. I think it was the best food I had ever eaten. I didn't realize we had not eaten in a while, and we had just been going on adrenaline.

The burger place was packed too. I began to look at the faces of the people around us. They all were tired and at the end of their ropes from the ordeal. No one had a destination, it seemed.

One very large, bald-headed man—looked like he might be a strong, tough, oil field roustabout—stood at the ice dispenser and started yelling at his son, "Where is my cup? Where is my cup?"

His young son lovingly said, "Dad, it is in your hand."

The man, realizing he was holding his cup, gently began to cry.

At another table sat a family—an older man and his wife, and a younger man and his wife. From their unique accent, you could tell they were from New Orleans. The older man appeared to have Parkinson's disease because he shook ever so slightly. The older woman began to cry out, "Where will we go if our house is flooded? Where will we go? I am too old to start over. I was raised in that house."

Again she asked, as if there were no one else in the room, as if she were all alone, "Where will we go, where will we go?"

The young man tried to offer support, but the older lady cried louder and was not to be comforted. Loudly, she began to wail, "Why God, why God . . . why?" Her crying was just uncontrollable.

I looked around the restaurant and saw many people had begun to cry too. I wondered how many had lost their homes or had lost loved ones in the storm. The air conditioning was the only sound you heard when the lady quit crying.

I looked over at Joseph, and he was crying too. He looked at me and said, "Let's go find some gas."

When we returned to the car, our gas needle was on an eighth of a tank. We still had 183 miles left to travel. Again I thought that we were not going to make it. I tried to hide my concern. As I cranked the car, I said, "Maybe we should turn the air conditioning off to save some gas."

Joseph, with a smile, said, "Ardie, what did I tell you? Have faith! Let's go! Let God find us gas!"

I still did not share Joseph's faith. I finally said, "Old man, unless we have a miracle, we are going to run out of gas. On the way down, there was no gas. Look at all of the parked cars on the side of the road. Has it dawned on you why they are there? They are out of gas. We passed seven gas stations, all out of gas. People were littered all around the station in hope of when they do get gas, at least they would be in position."

Joseph started humming some Gospel song. He was starting to piss me off.

I thought to myself, "I might be able to make it to Alexandria. It's a lonely stretch of road surrounded by cotton fields and soybean fields. Should I try? Just one more station before decision time."

As we approached, I saw that station was out of gas. Then, I looked to my left and saw what appeared to be a second gas station, a BP-84, also closed. But a man was walking from his office to the pump, and he looked as if he were turning the pump on.

I did a quick u-turn and asked the man, "You wouldn't by chance have gas?"

He smiled, "Son, this is your lucky day. I have been gone, but I am back now, and I think I still have some old gas in these pumps."

A state trooper heard my conversation, and he rushed over to the pump and said, "If there is gas, I have to have it first."

I prayed out loud while Joseph laughed. I prayed the trooper would not take all the gas, and I prayed I wouldn't kill Joseph.

I was able to get ten gallons. A line formed after us very quickly and in very disorderly fashion. The state trooper had to call for back-up. All I wanted was to get on the road.

I quickly pulled away from the station. Joseph just smiled as he said, "Turn the air conditioning on high."

I was glad he went quickly to sleep. As we passed Frogmore Plantation, I watched Joseph sleep.

I performed the eulogy at Joseph's funeral. I told everyone of his faith. The night of the New Orleans Saints' super bowl victory, I felt Joseph's spirit. I remember him saying, "Have some faith."

I thought to myself, "Sometimes our greatest blessings can appear oh, so, humble."

I'm Dying—What Shall I Wear?

Karen was a beautiful woman. She resembled Mrs. Robinson in the movie, "The Graduate." She spoke with a classic southern accent, but more slowly.

To Karen, the word "ham" could have three syllables. The first time I met her she offered up some of her southern wisdom. She said, "We have lots of crazies in our town. The trick is to stay on their good side, and for heaven's sake, stay away from the gun-toting crazies."

I tried desperately to follow her wisdom.

Over the years, I developed an odd relationship with Karen. After my first formal meeting and conversation, she called on me with a strange request. "Ardie," she said, "Please knock down my door. I have locked my keys in my house, and I am late for my card party." I quickly assessed the situation and reassured her that breaking down the door would not be necessary. I went to the back of her house and removed a pane of glass. I then lifted the window, climbed in, and walked through her house and opened the door to a befuddled Karen. With a childlike coyness, she said, "Ardie, it is disturbing how quickly you broke into my house, but I find your blue-collar manner refreshing. I am late for my party. I got to go."

My relationship with Karen normally involved doing small odd jobs and light chores in her home or yard. Karen had a most unique approach to horticulture. She felt that plants were never to be watered by artificial means. As she would say, "If they can't survive on their own, to hell with them! Only the strong survive, just like people."

Karen was a survivor herself. She had overcome much adversity in her life. Karen believed in God, but she would say, "I am not churchy. A lot of folks go to church to dress up and be seen. A lot of them are real hypocrites. I try to be good." We would often talk about various topics, but I would always try to inject God into our conversations. Once I posed the question, "Karen, after that, what?"

With a puzzled look, she retorted, "What do you mean?"

I clarified, "What I mean is after you achieve all in this world, after that, what?"

She thought for a moment, took a sip of iced tea and said, "Now that is a real mystery. A lot of folks have the traditional view of life, and then heaven or hell, but what I believe is personal." She continued, "What I believe is what I believe and it is special for me. I don't like to speak to others about this most personal matter."

Karen was a great card player, and she never showed her hand or opened up on her personal views of what "after that" meant, no matter how hard I pressed.

My last visit with Karen was bittersweet. I knew she was near the end. Always the Southern lady, she said she had arranged her funeral, she had chosen the clothing she was going to wear. She had pre-written her obituary, and she had even arranged for the caterer. She took comfort in knowing that she had her affairs in order. In what was to be my last goodbye, I remembered that I slowly walked from her room.

I turned back and watched her with her compact reapplying her lipstick and double checking her makeup. Karen died a week later.

How fitting that she was laid to rest under a large magnolia tree on that cold winter day. Karen would have loved the fact her funeral was well attended. What would have given her great joy was to know how well everyone was dressed. She would have smiled to know the fried chicken and potato salad was delicious and the desserts were to die for.

Heaven's Calling—No Roaming Charges

Liz was temporarily put into a foster home as a child, although both of her parents were alive.

Her mother had become quite ill, and her dad had his hands full with his work and raising his other children.

When I met Liz, she was fifty-eight, but obviously her childhood experiences had greatly impacted her life. It was the first thing she told me about herself. And it was due to her childhood fears that she said she always slept with the light on and was a very tactile person. Most often, she touched people's arms or held their hand as she spoke with them. It wasn't a flirty or sexual gesture, just a touchy one.

Liz described herself as very loving, but "On the other hand," she said, "cross me, and I can be quite volatile. Just love me and I will love you back." Liz was the type of person who had to lay down ground rules for new people she met, just as she did with me.

When Liz was diagnosed with breast cancer, her sister, Jackie, someone I had met through the church, insisted that she talk with me. "Unless you are a head shrink, don't try to get in my head," she said when I first went to visit with her. She explained further, "I will talk with you only because Jackie recommended I do so. Understand you are not my confessor; you are only here to visit with me." I assured her I would talk but mostly listen.

Although Liz appeared cold and direct, she was really neither. She had a warmth about her that just took a little while to surface. Once it did, she seemed almost childlike. Her bark was, indeed, greater than her bite. And, she was highly intelligent.

Liz had been raised in a devoted Christian family, but over the years her own pilot light for God and religion had been extinguished.

She was a great lover of science. She loved to talk about black holes and the big bang theory. These topics intrigued her and gave her a feeling of extraordinary excitement. She boasted about her Darwin fish on her car and the reactions it spurred when she drove on the freeway. Once she asked me, "How can a thinking person believe in a fairy tale which involves a god that made the world in six days? Must have been long-ass days, eh?" She felt that "believers" were nonsensical and totally delusional. She said, "Those people are the same type of people who created the tooth fairy, Santa Claus, and such."

She particularly detested television preachers. She made fun of the way they talked and asked me, "Why do those preachers talk so funny? When I was young and stupid and still a believer, I don't remember being taught that Jesus talked that way." But it seemed she might still have a question, a bit of an opening in her mind if I could answer her question, "If there is a god, why would he or she or it allow so much suffering?"

I never had the right answer.

One visit, after I had read up on the big bang theory, I confronted her with a question myself. "As a person of science," I began, "I am sure that you might be able to answer why, at the time of the big bang were there only trace elements like hydrogen, oxygen, etc.? If I understand the theory correctly, isn't it thought that it is from those elements, those base origins, that the perfect order of our world, our bodies, came into being?" I told her if she believed this she had taken a bigger leap of faith than I had.

I was not going to win any debates with Liz. She had greater cerebral capabilities than I. Moreover, I was not going to push faith down her throat.

I visited Liz shortly after her double mastectomy. She never looked so sad, so depressed, so lacking of joy. She quietly asked if I would hold her hand. We sat in silence for several minutes and she gently began to cry. "I was never beautiful—cute maybe, but not beautiful. Now, I am not anything. I am no longer a woman," she cried. No words I could say could give her hope or comfort. Although I thought Liz was beautiful, she did not feel beautiful.

Several weeks went by. I was checking the mail at the post office when my cell phone rang, and it was Liz. She sounded drunk, but explained that she was on heavy medication. She said, "I am scared." Then she asked, "Would you please pray for me?" I paused, and answered, "Why don't we pray together?" She replied, "You start." So I said, "Heavenly Father," and she repeated, "Heavenly Father." I don't recall the rest of the prayer we said, but when we hung up, I noticed that eleven minutes had elapsed on my cell phone.

The next day, Jackie called and said that Liz had died.

There was an elaborate funeral for her. The church was packed. A priest conducted the service, and a blues guitarist sang a tune. There wasn't a dry eye in the place. During the service, I laughed out loud when six cell phones went off all at the same time. Obviously, some people were just too embarrassed to pick up their cell phones to answer or turn them off. Liz would have smiled.

Don't Be a Wuss. Be a Man.

It was a cold day in February when a business associate of mine asked me if I would visit a dying friend of his. "Of course," I said. "Where is your friend, and what is his name?" I was shocked when he said the name. "Oh my God," I thought, "it's Coach O'Donnell, my junior high school football coach." When my friend told me his name, my head began to hurt because back in junior high, when someone messed up, he would hit them on the forehead.

Coach O was the premier alpha male, part drill instructor, part bad-ass dude. The guy used to scare the holy crap out of me. If you looked up the expression "hard ass," it would have his picture by the definition.

I had not seen Coach in forty-three years. What could I possibly say to him? Should I confess I put hand soap in his burger in 1967 . . . that I let the air out of his tires in 1968? What words could I offer that would give comfort to this dying man? Did I secretly want to spit in his face?

Coach O'Donnell was on the cancer wing in room G340. As I approached the room, I could see a small man lying in a bed. Surely, this was not the Coach I knew. He was much too small. I bit my lip, gathered my courage, and entered the room. The man I remember as six feet eight inches and 290 pounds of total muscle was no longer a giant. Instead, he was yellow, with yellow eyes, and he weighed maybe 150 pounds. The cancer had taken a toll on him.

"Coach O'Donnell?" I sheepishly asked.

"Yes," he said, with a voice as robust as I remembered.

"Coach, you don't remember me," I said, "but you were my gym teacher and coach in junior high."

He smiled and said he remembered me, but he really didn't.

Coach had been fired for being too hard on the kids. Some folks thought him cruel. Although I admit he was a tough old bird, strangely I always liked him.

In a clumsy manner I asked, "Are you at peace with God?"

He said, without hesitation, "Oh yes." He continued, "If you knew me then, you knew I was hard, punishing, and unforgiving. The truth is I wanted you kids to do your best, to be your best. The world is damned cruel and only the strong survive. I was teaching kids to learn how to deal with the hard knocks life sends your way. God reads hearts, and He knows I was not out to befriend you kids, but to turn boys into men. I know I had my faults, and maybe I was too tough. But God knew what I was trying to do."

I thought for a moment and said, "I cannot sit in judgment. All I know is you taught a lot of us to go the extra mile. To many, you motivated and strengthened us. On behalf of those boys who are now men, we thank you."

He began to cry. I could not stand to see him cry. I shook his hands; our eyes met, and I said, "Goodbye."

As I walked from the room, he said, "Tell Bourgeois, 'hello.'" I couldn't believe it. He did remember me.

When I was fourteen, I wanted him to burn in hell. Not anymore.

♪♪♪♪

Okay, okay, so you don't want me to mention Jesus.

On occasion, I am asked to come out and speak with a dying person, and I get a strange request. The loved one of the person dying will say, "Please don't mention Jesus." I used to ask why but not anymore. I get this request not just from nonbelievers or my yamaka-wearing friends, but from some who claim to be Christian.

When I hear this request, I realize the Christian community has done a poor public relations job for Jesus Christ. I admit I too am guilty.

I once shared a ski lift with a lady at Alta Ski Resort in Salt Lake. On the ride up, we talked. She told me she was out in Utah attending a funeral. She told me the funeral was at a Methodist church. I asked her if she was a Methodist, and she said, "Hell no." I asked her what her denomination was. I thought her response odd. She said, "I am certainly not a Christian. I am no asshole." I never put the two together.

The mention of God's name can be a put off for some folks. Nothing, and I mean nothing, generates a more visceral or divisive response from some folks than the mention of the name Jesus. Once I was visiting a man in his early fifties who was dying of cancer. Every other word out of his mouth cursed God, especially Jesus. I asked him why he was so mad at God and Jesus. He told me God and Jesus were the reason for all the hate, wars, and discord in the world. He thought anyone who claimed to be a believer was part of the grand conspiracy against mankind. I wondered what had shaped his thought and drove him to this conviction. I hate to say it but more and more people think ill of the followers of the Prince of Peace.

Should Christians be more humanitarian?

I know life begins with an orgasm.
And, I truly believe that our good Lord will top that feeling at our journey's
end.

Afterword

We are all going to die. The dying process is different for each person.
It can happen suddenly, or fill hours and days.
The dying experience is unique to you and will only take place at the
appointed time.
Your process of dying can be your life's ultimate purpose.
Others who share your dying will be forever changed.
What makes dying unique is not totally of this world . . . it touches the next.

If you are nearing
the end of your journey
and you come to the realization . . .
there is something
greater than yourself.

If you cry out and say, "God,
use me, guide me, direct me."
The God of the universe
will come.

God will take you to a wonderful
place where happiness
abounds . . .
where you can be happier than
you have ever been.

He will not come if you don't want Him.

Everyone can use a friend at the end.

It matters little what you believe. We all need to die with dignity and respect. I am often with people who are free thinkers, agnostics, atheists, republicans, or democrats. It does not matter. I believe everyone deserves to have comfort at the end. We are never to judge, but rather we are only there to comfort. To listen and learn.

Of course, if I can, I will remind someone if they want to go to God's heaven, they have to go by God's plan.

If they do not accept my message, it is their decision. I cannot judge. I believe this is only God's work. My nonbelieving friends feel there is no judgment.

We all will learn the great mystery one day.

♪♪♪♪

When I was ill as a child, my mother would wipe my face with a cool rag.
Saint Veronica was very bold; she risked her life to wipe the face of Jesus.
Good mothers are a lot like Veronica.